JOURNEY TO THE CENTER OF MY MIND

- A Single Volume

Author Contact:

pattiekake@earthlink.net

Publisher Contact:

info@roguescholars.com

Designed by C. D. Johnson
Cover design by Patricia Carragon

ISBN: 0-9774022-9-0
ISBN 13: 978-0-9774022-9-8

Produced By Rogue Scholars Press
New York, NY - USA

Journey to the Center of My Mind

Patricia Carragon
3/16/13

Poetry by Patricia Carragon

Produced By Rogue Scholars Press
http://www.roguescholars.com

I dedicate this book to Nomad's Choir, the Pink Pony West, Poet to Poet, Poets Wear Prada, the Riverside Poets, the Saturn Series, the Brooklyn poets and my loved ones and friends who helped to make this journey possible.

A special thanks to David Elsasser, DeeAnne Gorman, Leigh Harrison and Evie Ivy for their editorial guidance.

FOREWORD

A word about Patricia Carragon...

Early in 2003, as a regular attendee at the Pink Pony reading hosted by Jackie Sheeler, it was easy to spot the new kid on the block. First off, Patricia sat at a table of 4 by herself and warned me that she was expecting friends and if I wanted to sit there it was ok as long as I didn't mind a crowd showing up. She's new, I remember thinking, I wonder what her poetry is like. She had that antsy excitement of someone who of course can't wait for her time at bat in the open mike. I recall how charming it was to be caused to remember my first time reading on the circuit at the Garden at 6th Street and Avenue B, wanting to carve a place in a marvelously populated new world, surrounded by talent, wondering if I could fly.

That night at the Pink Pony was the start of what is turning out to be a truly exciting career for Patricia and the poets and listeners who have the luck to attend any of her performances. I use the word performance specifically for this spitfire of a woman who will storm onto the stage and give her 100 percent every time. Patricia Carragon is a spirited and enticing poet. Her writing explores emotion as a subject, working through insights that touch us all in ways ranging from her darkest moments to the wildly comic. Her joy of writing is easy to embrace and one wants to join her entourage straight away.

Patricia is one woman who will keep the fires of poetry well tended with this, her first book of poems, and over the years with many more writings and performances to come.

- Su Polo, Curator, Saturn Series Poetry Reading, NYC, October, 2005

CONTENTS

Journey to the Center of My Mind

Chapter 1 The Loner Within   PAGE

The Puppeteer   - October 2000   1
The Ivory Tower   - May 2003   2
Blue Fire   - October 2003   2
Emptiness   - January 2004   3
Sensuality   - May 2005   4
Secrets   - August 2002   5
Stain   - March 2003   6
Hello   - February 2002   6
The Bride Wore Black   - February 2004   7

Chapter 2 Anger, Inc.

Dirty Secret   - March 2003   9
Honesty   - May 2002   9
Rage   - June 2004   10
Touched By a Guide   - January 2003   10
Dirty Trick   - September 2003   11
Revenge   - August 2002   11
Tenderness in Reverse   - September 2003   12
Flying   - March 2003   12
Normal People   - July 2002   12
Metamorphosis   - March 2003   13
PMS Pizza   - October 2004   14

Chapter 3 The Flame and the Heart

The Eyes of Love   - January 2004   15
Universe In Motion   - August 2002   16
Yo Soy Una Persona Aislada   - June 2002   17
The Pixie   - October 2002   18
Blessed Stranger   - December 2002   19
Put Your Head Inside Your Heart - April 2002   19
The Dance   - January 2003   20
Vixen in the Rough   - January 2002   21

CONTENTS Continued

Chapter 4 Beyond Tears   PAGE

   Scars   – October 2003   23
   Erased By Myself   – January 2003   23
   Teardrops on My Pillow   – October 2002   24
   Observation Deck   – February 2003   24
   Forgotten Child   – November 2002   25
   Dead Flower   – February 2002   25
   Fit for a Child   – September 2003   26
   Baby Dolls   – May 2003   27
   The Valley of Sorrows   – June 2000   28
   In Death's Bed   – December 2001   29
   The Golden Door   – December 2004   30

Chapter 5 Attitude is Courage

   Revolution   – July 2000   31
   Twins   – January 2003   31
   X   – January 2002   32
   The Lioness   – January 2002   33
   Fire   – June 2004   34
   Vocal Minds   – June 2002   34
   The Elastic Canvas   – November 2000   35
   Unknown Minutes   – December 2001   36

Chapter 6 Dreams

   Eternal Sleep   – September 2000   37
   Phoenix of Light   – November 2003   38
   The Hole   – September 2002   39
   The Door   – April 2003   40
   Twilight   – September 2001   40
   Daydreams   – July 2002   41
   Crucifixion   – August 2002   41
   Humoresque   – March 2003   42
   Dreamscape   – October 2002   43

CONTENTS Continued

Chapter 7 Modern Life   PAGE

The Goddess   - June 2000   45
Little Girls   - May 2005   45
Tell Me a Story   - November 2003   46
Simplicity   - July 2002   46
The Spiral   - November 2002   47
The Asylum   - March 2001   47
Instant Coffee   - September 2003   47
Tension   - January 2004   48
Queen Bee   - August 2000   49
Truth   - February 2003   50
The End   - April 2001   50
End of an Error   - November 2002   51
Generic Religion   - July 2002   52
God and TV   - June 2004   52

Chapter 8 Miscellaneous Musings

At the Edge   - September 2003   53
The Empty Hall   - April 2001   53
Art of Lies   - July 2003   54
Lost and Found   - June 2003   54
Zero   - July 2002   54
Special Delivery   - September 2003   55
Egg   - June 2003   55
Tears   - December 2003   56
Indigo   - February 2003   57
The Opening   - March 2002   58
Random Thoughts   - June 2003   58
Final Words   - October 2002   59

Alphabetical Appendix

Patricia Carragon is a regular participant of the Poet to Poet Reading Series as well as the Saturn Series at the Nightingale Lounge in the East Village, the Pink Pony West Reading Series at the Cornelia Street Cafe and The Back Fence, both located in Greenwich Village, The Dactyl Foundation for the Humanities in SoHo and the Park Slope Poetry Project in Brooklyn.

Rogue Scholars and Poets Wear Prada have published her poetry on-line. Her work can also be found in such poetry journals as Nomad's Choir, the Park Slope Poetry Project's "Erato" and ABC NO RIO's "Stained Sheets."

She is co-hosting the Park Slope Poetry Society at the Spoken Words Café in Brooklyn with Evie Ivy. She is also one of the hosts for the ABC NO RIO Reading Series on the Lower Eastside.

Patricia's poetry was conceived and born in Astoria, Queens and nurtured by Brooklyn poets as well as others from the New York area. For her, poetry allows the imagination to guide the hand in writing down the voice from within. Poetry is a safe flight into her darkest moments and other forbidden territories with her at the controls. By using words on paper, they become puppets. Through these puppets, she can express any deep-rooted fear or desire without submitting herself to embarrassing conversation. She prefers to get things down on paper as a catharsis for the soul. These emotions and ideas, whether they are dark or light are beautified and the afterimages that they produce are rewarding and uplifting.

Please share her experience and take a journey to where the intelligence of the heart can contemplate the complexities of the mind.

Chapter 1
The Loner Within

The Puppeteer

The guardians of night make way for the day shift
To draw dawn's curtain at the end of the last act;
The marionettes take their final bow
At the final period of their performance.
They walk off the stage of lined paper,
Disappear into hallways of the puppeteer's mind,
Away from memory's spoken words
Written by the hand of the mute.

The puppeteer closes her pen
And is awed by her literary players
Who use body language as her voice,
Without erasing pride or intelligence.
She knows drama is a best kept secret
From certain critics who exaggerate
And thrive on others' misfortunes.
They enjoy the blunt edge of slander,
Brandish it as gossip that often slashes
And spills out indelible truths and lies
That never wash away.
This double-edge sword
Can cut out the tongues of victims,
Leaving them mute -
Never to speak of painful acts
That forced them to turn inward
And find the voice that was lost.

The puppeteer searched for many years
And found her voice through her puppets
Who convey her message on a paper stage.
She returns to the solitary seat
Reserved for her in the theatre of the night,
As the guardians of day make way for the night shift
To raise dusk's curtain at the start of the first act;
The marionettes take the stage
And the puppeteer opens her pen
For her voice to recite her story.

October 2000

The Ivory Tower

Hide me away up in the clouds,
Far from the twin worlds of kindness and hatred.
My days, numbered in bricks that were laid to rest
Before conception into a world where I am betrothed
To the whims of the quill, his fruits of frustration.
Inside this refuge of the unknown, I live and wait
For a purpose that cannot be resolved by anyone.
I sit up here, writing until the bricks decide to leave
For the phantom to find sanctuary from a memory
That never saw moonlight weep for her sun.

May 2003

Blue Fire

Blue fire,
Like a caged bird that wants to fly but can't,
Sings out loud on this winter's day.
Passion is her flame -
High-pitched in temperature,
Her fire stretches towards heaven.
So proud in form,
Like the lady who wears a cashmere coat
For a brief wintry stroll.

Blue fire,
Like icicles made from isolated tears,
Burns her skin as winter weeps.
The caged bird flies towards heaven -
Passion rips her wings,
Her fire falls to the ground.
Never hearing her song,
The lady predicts a winter's frost
Found in solitude.

October 2003

Emptiness

The empty room pretends to be what it's not -
A chamber full of exquisite possibilities.
But Gordian knots keep it unfulfilled,
Yet an empty chair does exist,
Occupying space.

Does it occupy its purpose
For an empty person to seek solace
In a crowd of inner space?

January 2004

Sensuality

She enters another dimension
Where sex becomes her muse.
Lust is just another foul flight
Into forbidden imagination
Where mystery sleeps with her incognito.

She dreams on, pretending
She is sensuality, the mistress of the heart -
The desire, the flame, the ultimate sin.
She dreams on, yet it's past midnight
And darkness is her only suitor.
He drapes a shroud over her shoulders,
Making her feel much colder than she is.
Her comforter slides to the floor,
Unwanted and unloved.

She rolls over, cries in echoes
That answer her vacuous words.
Loneliness recycles yesterday's trash
To be picked up by her pain
And repeat what was felt again and again -
Non-stop as darkness hugs her
Tighter and tighter.

She sees him as invisibility,
Touching her private identity.
His name is reality, the master of her mind -
The loss, the solitude, the ultimate punishment.
She dreams on, yet it's past three
And darkness is still her only suitor.
An empty chair is a witness
To the crime of her violation.

She becomes tired and surrenders to inertia -
She exits the dimension
For her eyelids to say goodnight,
Taking her home
To where sleep, the ultimate lover,
Waits for her prodigal return.

May 2005

Secrets

A woman sleeps alone
On a bed that provides no rest or comfort,
While a sleeping child is at peace
Inside her subconscious.
Adjacent to her bed is an empty vase
Stained with the image of hope.
Nearby, lies an unopened book
Bonded by her lifetime in words.
A window is open
For the wind to sneak in.

The telephone rings out of persistence,
Still, she hears nothing and remains incognito
Behind closed eyes sworn to secrecy,
Protecting her treasured yet troubled thoughts
From intruders who come to rob her intimacy.

She abruptly turns over on her singular bed -
The vase and book jump off the nightstand,
The telephone stops ringing and the wind exits.
The fallen book breaks its vow
And speaks for the first time,
Using tears shed from glass
To bookmark secrets on pages that cry
Like the child in her subconscious.

August 2002

Stain

The floor has no personality
But to a simple stain, it is home.
She can never aspire to rise above
To where noise would welcome her presence.
She lies alone, invisible tension from a terra unknown,
Inside a forest of legs whose laughter hides in vapors.

The fire is burning below, the floor feels her flames,
But the stain is quashed by the roots of her problems
Who stand tall with their heads fixed on indifference
And the comforts of wine and conversation
Cultivated from the firewood in the communal hearth.

March 2003

Hello

She prefers to sit alone
In an empty room on a broken chair
And listen to intelligent conversation inside her head
Instead of the nonsense outside her window.
She wages a losing battle,
A singular voice in coupled crowds -
Their strength is amplified in selfish valentines,
While she holds her broken heart and rose thorns.
Although their voices are muffled and hers is clear,
Her honesty loses impact amongst mindless cackles.

She closes her window, forgoing any hint of fresh air,
Since the pollution outside is greater than its welcome.
The clock's solitary chimes
Pose a disturbing reminder of what she has lost -
This obsession insinuates, like her rose thorns.
She reopens the window to rid herself of this nuisance
And deploys her protest as a "hello"
To the revelers below.

February 2002

The Bride Wore Black

The bride had no choice but to wear black on her wedding
    day -
Why wear white when it will show the dirt of a four letter
    word?
She walked down an aisle that was non-existent,
Carrying not a flower or even a weed as her bridal bouquet.
No guests were present to watch the solemn event,
Nor was there a groom to welcome her heart.
Even God was not around to witness her vow -
Solitude presided over the ceremony.

She said, "I do," blowing a kiss to herself,
Untouched by the consummation
Symbolized by a circle of gold.
The single woman was now married to herself,
For better for worse, for richer for poorer,
In sickness and in health, to love and to cherish,
Till death ...

February 2004

7

Chapter 2
Anger, Inc.

Dirty Secret

Behold the stain upon naked skin,
Orphaned filth spawned from cesspools of DNA.
Indelible evidence of what was, what is, what will be,
Untouchable and incompatible to the benefits of soap.
See how it freezes the fragile flesh I wear,
I cover it up with layers of protection,
Hoping to conceal it before wind rips them off.

The truth will be arrested, tried without a jury,
The verdict read by the Devil's advocate.
My privacy will hang by the noose,
Shadows will bow their heads in prayer
Before being stepped on by curious soles,
When the hour hand reaches out to heaven
As clouds look down out of curiosity.

March 2003

Honesty

Poison has a way of camouflaging itself,
Wearing sugar-coated clothing
While administering itself as medicine.
Doses of criticism and advice
Cure the egos of those who watch
Your self-esteem self-destruct into dust.

Call it honesty, but I call it destruction
When in the wrong hands
Becomes toxic like human neglect.
It poisons every element of life
Until you surrender all that you have,
Succumbing your naked thoughts
To be scattered at the feet of victors,
Leaving you, the sole victim,
Homeless, without solace in defeat.

May 2002

Rage

Betrayal stabs you in the heart,
Trinitarian walls condense your worth
Leaving little space to breathe.
Smoke filters past air ducts,
Rises to your head,
Smashes the window of your third eye,
But you still can't find your way out.
Visions of life pass your doorway
But refuse to enter.
You are a caged animal on fire
In an isosceles world of imperfection,
On view to be forgotten
Until your heart implodes
Forms a dark cloud of ash,
Ready to attack the sunshine
In a crash of thunder.

June 2004

Touched by a Guide

The years of time are heavier than they look -
My shoulders feel every kilo of day and night
Spent under the tutelage of your provident patience
Until pressure cracked my senses, like brittle bones.
You watched evidence twist into a transfiguration,
A monster contrived to dwell as an aberration
Inside your Garden of Eden that has grown barren
Where the guilty one was singled out as female.
You were acquitted to watch my life burn at the stake
By your hand that lit my funerary pyre.
But before I am consumed by hate and failure,
I want to blow embers to touch the one
Who guided me down the sacred path of deceit.

January 2003

Dirty Trick

Laughter applauds the humor of the act,
Magic plays a dirty trick on the magician -
In the finale, cuts him in half.

Congratulate yourself for the moment,
Toast yourself on your accomplishment -
This moment belongs to you, alone.

Drink up! The rest of time does not belong to you -
The contract was already signed by proxy.
Drink every red corpuscle of revenge -
Your last opportunity to kill his spotlight
Before applause leaves the theatre
For the stage to stand alone.

September 2003

Revenge

Porcelain egos crack faster than ordinary eggshells,
Aggravation burns the boundaries of logic to a crispy edge.
Hurt feelings pierce the perfect yolk and oozes out in pain,
Temperamental temperature causes the pan to smolder.
Panic rises and sets off alarms just as the pan jumps off the
stove,
Tossing well-done conversation to scatter across the kitchen
floor.

August 2002

Tenderness in Reverse

The fork and knife come forth to perform surgery
On a corpse that was once the pride of the farm.
The meat was cooked to perfection,
Bleeding slightly at each incision,
But tastefully tender in my mouth.
My tongue is in full motion
Mixing my thoughts between the molars
As they tenderize each morsel
For revenge to be properly served.

September 2003

Flying

Anger crosses a street at the intersection -
A vehicle takes flight into the cerebral dimension.
In full gear, it exceeds calculation -
The driver cannot drive when the mind does it all
Without maps of assistance on ethereal arteries.
It speeds past the nothingness of vague mist,
Exiting before that final leap
Where the outcome anticipates the passenger.

March 2003

Normal People

Routine demands order for a perfect world -
Acceptance is the rule for obedient subjects
Wearing invisible leashes along suburban streets.
Partnered members from Noah's great ship
Mortgage the American Dream
Inside identical boxes called "happy homes."

Fear the rejects who hate these very streets,
Walking single file past manicured tombstones
Where members from Noah's great ship
Hide behind paper-doll existence.
Fear the rejects who walk with insight

12

Among crowds of numbers and nonchalance.
Cameras will catch our anomalies
As evidence married to different values -
Our perspective vision will be subject to arrest.

Fear us because we live next door
And upstairs in the privacy of your bedrooms.
Fear us because our thoughts are spreading
From house to house, street to street,
Until time stands still for the fire to begin.

July 2002

Metamorphosis

Depression washes her face in the mirror,
Sadness stencils a metamorphosis.
Anger cracks it, capturing teardrops
Resembling albino blood on glass.

Her lair made a covenant with Nature,
Preparing a cocktail for sadistic pleasure.
Pain knits capillaries into tightened coils
Cut by monthly razors until they ooze,
Saturating a feminine network within.

Moonlight cascades on a sanguine web,
A spider emerges - her cycle begins.

March 2003

13

PMS Pizza

God hates women!
Pass the chocolate to my hips, please...
Before I kill you tonight.

Hormones go postal,
Estrogen pulls the trigger -
My body is target practice for pain.
But first, order me a pizza
With extra cheese for my cellulite
And a pepperoni phallus sliced for pleasure,
Because a hungry woman is dangerous
When her mood swings like the reaper.

PMS writes a postscript
For a rendezvous with my butt.
My tampon's sex drive,
A Pap Smear in drag,
Alerts me that the salsa is ready
And I want to die...

Maybe next week, I will crave something different,
Like love sandwiched in mocha mousse
Topped with Hershey Kisses.
But pass me another slice of pizza, please...
Before I kill you tonight.

October 2004

Chapter 3
The Flame and the Heart

The Eyes of Love

My eyes see nothing but time's empty room,
Covering the sheets of my introverted bed.
Misery needs a voice to be heard by cyber space -
I pretend to send out signals of genius to myself
For the quill is as dead as my previous incarnation.

Like genetics, I hold many secrets to be found
In cryptic letters written on glass beads
Strung on a chain, worn tightly around my neck,
Making it impossible for the story to be told.
I write in the past tense in conjunction with the future
Within the present tension of my presence,
Feeling smaller than a square foot of solitude,
My eyes too afraid to look.

Yet the words seem to know more than I:
When to elude inquisitive question marks.
But even more secretive than the story of my life
Is the one who wears the eyes of love.

I do not know him, but his eyes follow mine -
I will open my eyes and succumb to his power,
Seeing myself as I am for the first time,
If time would ever give me the freedom
To rip these beads from my neck
And watch them crash to the floor,
One by one.

January 2004

15

Universe in Motion

I began as nothing,
A lonely cell revolving around a secular axis
Shifting her course to whims of life and personal crisis.
My circumference shows depth from within,
Ready to accessorize accoutrements
Of pleasure and thought.
My table, laden with the finest linen,
China, silver and glass,
Acquired from a taste for knowledge
And necessity for spirit.
Within this solitary universe
I am the guest of honor and the hostess to none.
My food and wine sit in anticipation -
I admire their patience
And stare at a bowl of ripened fruit -
A centerpiece sweetened with a hunger
For life that wants to happen.

I rise from this festive table
And open the door for sunlight to enter my home.
I welcome him, like a friend,
And offer him my honored seat at the head of my table.
He is more than that
But rather an expansion of something released
After being asleep with silence for many years.
My room grows larger
And my home now has room for two.
This time, my universe expands for a purpose,
Not just for myself, but to share it with another
While standing independent in our merger.
We lift our glasses to toast our revolution in motion
As planets and stars outside the window
Watch us submerge into an astral sea,
Somewhere between the future and the unknown.

August 2002

Yo Soy Una Persona Muy Aislada

Yo soy una persona muy aislada
De donde la alegria no tiene entrada,
Y antes de acostarme quiero
Sentir tu corazón sincero.
Yo vengo de nada
Y hacia ti voy.
Rica soy entre los ricos -
En amor, amor soy.

I Am a Very Isolated Person

I am a very isolated person
From where happiness has no entrance
And before lying down, I want
To feel your sincere heart.
I come from nothing
And towards you I go.
I am rich amongst riches -
In love, I am in love.

June 2002

The Pixie

Your unusual eyes
Pull me beneath covers of imagination.
You make your bed in a new world
Situated on the shoulders of your small frame.
Call me your beautiful sad-eyed friend,
A woman lost in time and space.

I am learning, moving in a trance, hearing your story,
Not meant to be read to children at night
But to an adult who needs to feel words
Best described when the lights go to sleep.
This secret ceremony seeks consummation -
Nocturnal rhythms walk together
Along a path paved with stars,
Guiding us into happiness' light,
Moving faster and faster,
Until my fear of losing you throws me off course.

Please hold me tight,
I am falling from this height of pleasure,
Afraid that I am destined to land
In some nameless place where my worst fears
Will seize me, take me back to a former life -
Forever lost, never to see the gentle waterways
Flow from your unusual eyes,
Forever lost from the magical touch
Revealed by your storyteller's heart.

October 2002

Blessed Stranger

I love you, whomever you are,
A stranger from a distant minute
From another time which became today -
A gentle stranger with friendship in his eyes.
Your name is not important
Since I already know you,
When yesterday belonged to wishes
Long lost in the present grind,
Manipulated by hatred's hands.
Still, I find that your loving hands
Caress the compassion of my heart.
Come take me blessed stranger
And let us fly together as one
Where the universe travels faster
Than the celestial pace of dreams at night.
Let our bliss multiply among stars
With the excitement of fireworks,
Kissed by the spirit,
Taking us to that higher octave
On the scale of love.

December 2002

Put Your Head Inside Your Heart

Put your head inside your heart -
This is where it belongs.
Put your eyes inside your heart -
The reflection of love
Can never be distorted.
Put your voice inside your heart -
It must never rise
To threaten the dawn.
Put your body inside your heart -
The dawn awaits her lover,
Knowing that in the morning
Your heart will rise in peace.

April 2002

19

The Dance

The dance begins,
The passion is lit.
The fire consumes,
The pleasure is hot.
The castanets arouse,
The allegro is alive.
The guitar makes love,
The crescendo is met.
The dance slows down,
The music is humming.
The passion whispers,
The dawn is anxious.
The candle blows out,
The fire is gone.
The castanets lie still,
The guitar is at rest.
The dancers unlock,
The kiss, their samba.

January 2003

Vixen in the Rough

The woman is a magician -
She undresses the conjugal bed
And seduces her mate.
He falls into her trap beneath innocent sheets
Made from the finest cotton threads.
She heats up passionate crescendos
Until her fever becomes bored
And loses hunger for his masculine fuel.

Forgive my intrusion,
But I see this scenario
Like an erotic kaleidoscope
Who undresses your secret under covers.
You may not think of me as an obscenity
Confined in her abstention from touch,
Yet I am a vixen in the rough -
A wild child trapped inside a spark
Waiting to strike the magic
For heaven to explode into flames.

January 2002

Chapter 4
Beyond Tears

Scars

How does one hide from oneself
Etched in broken sidewalks of hands?
Like scars carved by an unknown artist,
Skin reveals a twisted passage
Where the tree of life grows out of cracks,
Strives toward a destination that cannot be seen
By either sky or earth.
Its roots are broken from earlier traumas,
Yet they persist in growing as scars across our palms.
We must learn to hide our hands in lies,
Hoping that our deformities will never be trampled upon
By the evidence that walks between the cracks.

October 2003

Erased By Myself

In the bathroom, a hot shower breathes
On the mirror of a medicine cabinet -
The glass disappears into silver mist,
My face is erased by moisture.
My purification demands a bar of soap
For a burnt offering wrapped in a towel
To take a sacrificial shower,
Only to emerge out of the steam
Still drenched in yesterday's filth.

January 2003

23

Teardrops on My Pillow

Salt water slips past a broken duct,
Stains muslin innocence.
Drams of worry disturb peace,
Defeat is the echo inside my head.
My private hell has gone public,
Evidence rests on my pillow
For darkness to witness drama
In the first act.

October 2002

Observation Deck

I see the world as incredible deception
From my peak of isolation.
Alone, observing the four faces of myself,
I contemplate and reflect on each direction -
North, south, east and west.

Polarity is no longer a compelling thought
When distance stretches its arms between us -
Opposites do not come together
To touch philosophical innocence.
But destruction has shaken my foundation
By a fault that moved you further away from me.
I turn my head to the east and to the west -
From where the sun rises and falls,
Wondering if I should leave my haven -
A purgatory's nest for an eagle with broken wings,
Too injured to fly where the sun never falls.

I forfeited my life to the four faces of myself,
Distanced from your face.
Alone, looking to the north and to the south,
I hide myself here in the apex of intellect
While my ego descends to the four directions -
North, south, east and west;
Never to know how you are observing the distance
That blocked us from our points of view.

February 2003

Forgotten Child

Her eyes once glowed with the future
That came and went without notice.
A broken mirror remembers too well
The forgotten child who ran away
From a life that changed the image
Caught in a reflection of thought
Between past and present.

November 2002

Dead Flower

I may be fluent in maturity,
But I am still a child
Who walks awkwardly in high heels
And lifts the hem of her over-sized skirt.
No language written or spoken
Can ever fully translate this rotten mood.
In adult clothes, I speak adult words,
Pretend to take the stage in an adult world.

Yet I am still a child,
Who holds a wilted flower
And hides her personal shame,
Fearing that at any moment,
Seams will suddenly expose
The dried petals of a fairy tale princess
Who forgot how to cry.

February 2002

Fit for a Child

One night I entered a dream,
Past the music, to a room fit for a child,
A female haven for pretending -
A little table stands at attention,
A chair in its designated spot,
A napkin folded in a perfect triangle,
A teapot to pour make-believe into delicate cups,
A cake layered in pink sweetness
Regally placed before a plate, knife and fork
For the guest to be served.

I took my reserved seat at the place of honor
To partake of this ritual set before me.
Across from my view, a miniature kitchen set -
A sink flowed fantasy from its faucet,
A refrigerator preserved milk and eggs for play,
An oven and stove pulled magic tricks
From tiny pots and pans.

I was amazed at what I saw and forgot who I was.
My joy expanded like a party balloon,
Seeing a little image of love
Seated in a highchair in the corner -
A baby doll with a perfect smile
Sealed with plastic promise of the ever-after.
I walked over to pick her up,
Just as I would have done
When I was in proportion with this room,
But the dream vanished into my pockets.

The room aged in years -
The table was barren, except for dust,
Crumbs have gone into the mouths of disgust,
China and flatware, pots and pans lay broken and bent
In a sink where the faucet has gone dry.
Milk was missing from the refrigerator shelf
While a few eggs sit in limbo,
A stove and oven too weak to perform magic.

The doll matured with the room -
Her smile faded,

Her face, no longer smooth, but wrinkled.
The highchair, her first seat in life,
Was ready to take her to the exit.
I tried to comfort my loss,
Listening to the walls of silence -
A silence too real, too honest and too much.

September 2003

Baby Dolls

Light the match, the baby dolls are crying -
Throw the match in, the pyre waits to be fed.
Burn tender flesh made from porcelain and vinyl
Until the whimpers of tiny voices are hushed
By cradled hands of flames.

Watch smoke shake apart a veiled room,
A celestial crib built from dreams left to rot.
The pyre picks the bones of unleavened ash,
Eulogizing a maternal heart laid to rest.

May 2003

The Valley of Sorrows

She walked through a valley of sorrows
Where children sleep beneath monuments
Engraved by broken illusions of toys
And fairytales that never came true.
The valley still wet,
Not from rainfall or a gardener's hose,
But from the tears of memories
Buried in practical bodies of adulthood.

She walked past monuments,
Stopping by one
Which bore her name.
A plaintive cry ran static electricity
Between herself and an emerging image
Of a familiar face
That used to be hers long ago.
It did not matter
Whether the cry was from her
Or from the apparition
Since they merged into one -
Uniting past with present,
Child with adult.

Her eyes conveyed many secrets -
Hammering of hands,
Stabbing of tongue,
Bruises tattooed as invisible scars
That never heal.
Stigmatas of pain bestowed on her
Not by her will, but by parental anger,
Searching to solve problems.

Flashes of childhood skipped past her,
Awakening memories of other children.
Picture books of horror
Colored the atmosphere -
Abuses ranging from gray to black,
Verbal to sexual, similar or worse,
Still haunt this sanctum for innocent tears.

Wails grew louder
To deafen the woman's cry for help,

But she is tired of mourning
When memories keep this cemetery moist.
Her past must remain
Where children sleep beneath monuments
Engraved by broken illusions of toys
And fairytales that never came true,
Knowing the future digs her grave
On the other side of the hill.

June 2000

In Death's Bed

In Death's bed I lay my weary head to rest -
My body heavy from the strains of stress
That paint my sky in rainbow delusion
To blend with the monotones of my life.
Let me lie here in peace
And be seduced by darkness
Somewhere between black and white.

But memories form a circle
Like taunting school girls:
My past, present and future hold hands,
Sing life's nursery rhymes
In an endless sing-song
That menaces my mind to tears.

Now my future breaks away
And darkness takes me into its arms,
Embraces me with compassionate peace
And promises a world where dust nor fire,
Rain nor wind, will never hurt me again.

December 2001

The Golden Door

The golden door is gone,
Light now covers its bones.
My question is no secret -
Did love die for me to live?

December 2004

Chapter 5
Attitude is Courage

Revolution

I will rise out of the zero of nothingness,
Take each radical step, degree by degree,
Rotate in full circle,
To complete a revolution
In three hundred and sixty degrees.

I do not care about images of perception
Created out of illusion
To shape me into the vision
Of what is best for me or worst for you,
Whether you are a friend or foe.
Yet friend and foe share both sides of the coin,
Purchase objects of possession,
Symbols of ownership and control.
But I am not for sale
And refuse to be part of the marketplace
For your inspection to place value upon me,
As you do for diamonds and stocks.

The mountain will come to me -
You shall crumble into pebbles
Over my self-evolution
As I ascend, fearless and strong.
I shall follow the calling within me,
Climb to my highest peak,
To fly with eagles and touch stars -
Free and powerful, like a pulsar,
Ready to revise unread chapters
And reclaim destiny upon this mountain,
Feeling fearless and strong.

July 2000

Twins

I am the glass that gives this window life,
Naked transparency born out of rock
For those who want to see through me.
I am confusion fused out of fragility and strength,
A master plan born from the architect's mind.
I am twin faces well versed in the tempest

31

That beats against the windowpane.

The window is closed,
But the turmoil outside is weak in comparison
To one erupting within this house.
My outer face is aware of cause and effect,
My inner one feels no air to sooth her cheek,
Recalls when paternal history cracked her
For being too expressive in opinion.

I am tired of guarding a lie -
A silent scream sends out a forceful gale
And disrupts orderly design and décor.
My primeval instinct still remembers
Being strong and tall above valleys -
A gust of heritage releases me,
No longer an image in glass
But one born of rock.

January 2003

""

My name's a chromosome, all female,
Lacking the "Y" to open doors.
Yet my name's the unknown,
Asking to be conquered,
Not by others, but by herself.

I'm part of an equation licensed to travel
Many times into endless prospects,
Galaxies for creative formula -
A seeker searching for solutions
To problems that keep doors closed.

My name's simple, but it's at the crossroads
Where I'm the point between two pyramids
In which earth and sky become my universe.

My name's "X," I sign it with pride.

January 2002

The Lioness

She moves with a symmetry all her own,
Paces back and forth like kinetic art framed by bars.
I see myself in her sultry yet intelligent eyes,
Yellow intensity in pools of irises.
The lioness believes my thoughts to be like her own -
Through her own telepathy, she commands,
"Get out, get out if you can!"

Sensing her thoughts to be identical to mine,
I approach the cage, fearless, yet gentle,
Clench the bars that separate animal from human,
I place my ears against the bars, await her next command.

The lioness stops abruptly, stares directly into my eyes
And demands, "Why do you stand here?
Try to get out if you can!
We are all animals and must follow our instincts...
It's our calling, but I'd rather consider it natural.
These bars keep the occupants on both sides in captivity
You've been domesticated too long
Watching my wild spark wither...
So please get out, get out if you can!"

At that moment, the beast becomes no different than I -
The fusion of bondage makes the lioness my twin.
The cage door thrusts open, her spirit jumps forward,
Not to eat me for fulfillment of survival,
But to feed me with her wild nature to become
The huntress of life.

January 2002

33

Fire

Hair is fire,
Thoughts turn crimson.

Lips speak scarlet,
Flames shout from pages.

An audience ablaze -
Words burn like sun.

June 2004

Vocal Minds

Can you hear the silent enemy
Attack you from within?
Can you feel your voice being sabotaged
By an unseen force that steals the courage,
Feeds your spirit to rebel?

Speak up if you want to be heard!
Your mind is shouting out loud
Before fear prepares you,
The guest of honor.

Your trepidation is hungry
And considers your dreams a delicacy
Along with your creative impulses.
They want to swallow all that is positive
In one powerful gulp
And leave your mind to waste
After the feast is over.

June 2002

The Elastic Canvas

I am lost inside this forest of easels,
Trying to motivate my canvas to life.
My fingers are wooden
Like these immobile sticks
That support wishful masterpieces
Created by brush strokes
From Michelangelo and Picasso wannabes
To draw praise from our teacher's perspective
For the coveted prize of "artist."

I am not entitled to call myself an artist -
My brush is as useless as my inspiration,
My blank canvas is nothing more
Than another self-portrait of how I feel,
Spending another lost hour in this forest
Where dense restrictions keep my true colors
Within guidelines perched upon sticks.

Yet my perspective is too peripheral
To remain prisoner to an easel,
Motivation crosses its edges
Much to the disapproval of my teacher
And his obedient audience.
It encourages me to toss my canvas
And leave the classroom -
No longer lost, but found.

November 2000

Unknown Minutes

Unknown minutes pave infinite tracks
For life's train to stop at different stations
According to our individual time tables.
We are travelers by nature,
Carrying instinctive desires
To pass through towns not found on maps.
We crave new experience,
Look at the landscape outside our window
And absorb the mobile moments.

But we are lured back to the train's course
Because we are conditioned to follow.
We are secured paupers
Rolling on endless iron -
Never having time to enjoy ourselves,
Yet rich enough to spend on regret.

Our train's destination is forever on schedule,
But for us, life and happiness are never on time.
We are tired of being faceless passengers
Riding, like cattle, on the rails of Fate.
We must stop wasting our unknown minutes,
Where days crowd into empty years.
Let's get off this train, take back what was lost
And turn our unknown minutes into pioneers
To show us worlds within ourselves.

December 2001

Chapter 6
Dreams

Eternal Sleep

Sometimes, I am still asleep
With both eyes open in a programmed world.
Rules and expectations implode my self-worth
Inside this vacuum,
Where I feel weightless as dust
Constantly swept away
By critical eyes.

I watch my dreams rise, stretch
And mimic me in the mirror across from my bed.
They slip out of their night clothes,
Dress in outfits suitable for the wide-awake
To join me for another day battling soldiers
Of the conscious world and everyday life.

The eyes of my subconscious world
See me as a robot in unhealed flesh.
They try to get my attention,
Spray paint optical illusions on walls -
But the illusions are not illusions.
The graffiti is more literal than visual -
Cryptic messages speak
And I must not be afraid.

A breath of dormant drama startles me
As the eyes of dreams merge with visible ones,
Become identical explosions inside a vacuum
And release dust into a magnificent vista.
My world of fantasy is becoming fact -
I see myself as I really am,
Throw my corrective lenses to the floor
And watch them smash into my galaxy of awe.
I see the planets, the stars and the sun -
I see myself as a woman... I see myself as me.

September 2000

Phoenix of Light

My body is reduced to a feather
Incapable of strength
Yet I am too heavy with grief
To escape panic's gaze.
Hell has sent its fury
To burn the eyes of heaven.
The innocent feels abandoned,
While God remains invisible.
Paralysis grounds me -
I do not deserve to die,
Nor do I deserve to live like this.

The past and future are frightened
And run towards me.
They know that I live only for the present
And understand they are also in danger
For I stand before the approaching peril,
Hypnotized by its imperious majesty.
I am just another target made of flesh -
Demons perfect their cruelty on me,
Destruction chews on bones
That once supported my innocence.

The past and future are nothing to me now,
Banging their heads against the concrete wall.
The fire calls me by my secret name,
The bull's-eye aims for penetration -
My mind is shattered glass.

The executioner is ready,
But the ax never falls.
A beam of light swoops down like a bird,
Snatches me from death's tentacles.
I want to merge into its power,
Which burns neither skin nor soul,
But I cannot trust its radiant show of faith
And have heard its music years before.

Should I opt for the fall
And hope to land somewhere
Within the catacombs of reason

Where the iconoclast lays hidden?
My decision hears my anguish
And waits...

November 2003

The Hole

The hole cuts a precise incision into the unknown
Where a passageway of questions takes the weary traveler
On a journey to find answers on the other side.
Whether it leads me to be welcomed by joyous prospects
Or be seized by the hands of misfortune's misfits,
I still have freedom to pursue my quest.
But this little hole which stands before me
Has darkness to guard both entrance and exit.
My finger cannot penetrate the chipped plaster -
The wall prevents me from searching further.
The hole smiles back at me with a victorious grin;
The winner, yes, as I back away, feeling smaller and
        emptier,
More hole-like than the mocking squatter
Who found a home on my two-dimensional wall.

September 2002

The Door

Hope is an artist who takes a canvas
Bathed in absolute darkness,
Draws an outline
And reveals a door etched in an aura of light.
The door beckons and draws me
To this self-portrait of anticipation;
It opens slowly to attract my anxiety -
I come closer like a moth in a trance
At the edge of dimension,
Attempt to stretch illumination
For the privilege of insight
And pass beyond the entrance
To become someone greater.

My fingers desire the subject
But the artist is disturbed,
Instructs the door to return to a still life
And slams my hand out of retaliation
As obscurity breaks the painful silence -
Shatters the cloistered halo
Around the blackened door
To fall to the floor like broken stars.

April 2003

Twilight

The noon sun watches from above
As the children pass a ball
Like minutes on a clock.
A figure draped in light's absence
Looks on from the side,
Sipping a glass of wine.
He watches childhood's game grow old
As the children become tired,
Knowing rest and comfort
Wait patiently in the shadow
Of his twilight's hour.

September 2001

Daydreams

Daydreams hide in storybook dialogue,
Never to be read when nighttime
Wakes subconscious evil
From cavernous sleep.
I close my eyes to read,
Seeing more in consecrated light.
You stand before me and I smile.
Scenes change,
But the actor remains the same
Until daydreams turn bittersweet,
For closure to destroy the end.

July 2002

Crucifixion

You come from nowhere -
An alien with a sense of precognition
Emerging out of innocent dreams best left
To storytellers who entertain the children born
Of children who still believe in the mystical promise,
Born out of hope and despair's wedlock.
We all are citizens from your place of birth;
Life is conceived from the same place.
Each day is a question that breeds another
Without any answers to stop them from coming
Since our stories are made-up by strangers
Secretly watching over us,
Passing judgment in their favor.
They prepare the lambs for their sins
While retribution retreats for a holiday
Far from the crucifixion of life
At the stroke of crisis.

August 2002

Humoresque

The ringmaster steps forward, identifies me in the
    darkness -
A criminal caught by fate and tried by limelight.
The circle enlarges on cue to delight a jury of fools,
Bedazzles impatience in the bleachers
That wear faceless questions adding humor to the skit.

The show begins with my life, juggling scenes in my head -
Clowns gather around me to see what's behind my
    make-up,
Snatch my face from underneath as I stand before the
    bleachers,

A naked dream in full exposure
To the heat of lupine drama starving for comic relief.
They laugh at me, pull my hair and toss water in my face
As bread and circus for hungry mimes of prey.
The final act serves its tart dessert.
They beat me with props until my pasty skin simulates
The polka dots on their costumes.

But the crowd is easily bored and demands more -
Clowns acquiesce out of fear and attach leeches to my
    psyche,
As if nakedness did not please such an eclectic group.
The crowd cheers to see my spirit's blood sealed with my
    name,
An aperitif to quench their thirst, paid in revenge.

You watch in horror from behind a torn curtain,
Seeing sacred appellation bleed from my eyes.
Your imagination steals me from the clutches of judgment,
On a stolen mare you ride into reality,
Take that leap through the proverbial "Ring of Fire"
And escape to that place where freedom paves the path
Far from the roar of the stampede.

March 2003

Dreamscape

Strange how when we go to sleep, we really do not sleep at
    all -
Relaxation is not always the time for a tired body to find
    peace
When a restless mind craves to wander alone at night.
The mind sees worlds similar and not so familiar,
Taking strange roads that never seem to end.
Each night, a road takes a different turn,
Going to places that have no borders,
Where signs speak in endless clues
To meanings, prophetic or not,
Camouflaged in scenery,
Whimsical, yet planned
To tease the mind
During "sleep."

October 2002

43

Chapter 7
Modern Life

The Goddess

The Goddess comes face to face with Herself
While applying Her morning make-up.
She colors Her bland complexion with sunlight
Until She is picture perfect,
Like a model in a magazine.
She admires Her retouched image,
Painted like a photographic portrait
By the reflective eyes of Her mirror,
And Her lifestyle, after a few moments,
Becomes a still life
On a candid canvas stretched from glass.
She studies the face of flawed Cubism,
Puts Her cosmetic case away,
Feeling not much better than She did
When She was just an ordinary woman
Living in a world of work and worry.

June 2000

Little Girls

What are little girls made of?

Sugared spice,
Oh so nice -
Wild cherries jubilee -
Shirley Temples,
Ruby Ritas,
Bloody Marys,
Frozen Margaritas.
Happy Hour cocktails -
Bitches in heat
Charm snakes and snails,
Wag puppy dog tails.
Sugared spice
With pigs in blankets -
Weenies roasted,
Nuts broken.

And that's how little boys think!

May 2005

45

Tell Me a Story

A child rises from a restless bed
With eyes older than her years.
"Please tell me a story," she requests,
And my little tale begins.

A simple story minus complicated ink spills
To spell out my fears -
A princess thinks she will find her prince
On the last page,
Filled with promises for a happy ending
Married to fabrication.

I know the truth will be too honest
For tender ears to hear my rage,
But her ears fool me with her innate ability
To translate contradiction.
She knows that a beast
Will eventually murder the princess in the end.

The sandman knocks,
The child embraces peace in her teddy bear's arms.
The lamp falls asleep and enters a world
Where it too can pretend.
My voice is lost in darkness,
A memory forgotten by the comforter.
The fairy tale exits with me -
The princess shall live to face another day.

November 2003

Simplicity

Survival bouncing from one side of your brain to the other,
Tight convolutions tie infinite knots in your stomach.
Choking fits dominate your will to find happiness,
Anger and loss compete for your gut.
Appointments for problems are forever on schedule,
No detours on unlimited highways to disaster.

Simplicity takes a holiday and sends a postcard.

September 2002

The Spiral

Walk away from the center of the labyrinth -
Begin at your pace until you grow into its intensity,
Stay at it while your mind slams at every twist and turn.
Keep walking until you complete your tedious journey,
Believing in your release from its enslavement,
Distanced from the core of being yourself
As the spiral wraps its hands around your neck,
Like a snake that craves dessert.

November 2002

The Asylum

The noise slams my head
Against stereo walls
Like fast balls
Pitched to home plate.
I cannot escape soon
From this tiny cocoon.
My battered body lies
On the solitary floor
Against the cranium door,
Waiting for sanity to return.

March 2001

Instant Coffee

Hurry up with the adrenaline rush of life
For the seconds are running faster and faster.
I'm out of breath maintaining this crazy pace,
Brewing magic crystals in my ceramic caldron.
Microwaves conjure a liquid spell
For instant gratitude substituted as pleasure.
I pretend to be larger than the molecules
Squirming in a heated bath that reinvents me
As my conquest before I'm conquered again
By the haste that cooks up the flavor of the day.

September 2003

47

Tension

Turn up the volume for drums
To beat your brain to a pulp

Fast forward your pressure
To amuse your boss

Be cloned in a Petri dish
To inherit more responsibilities

Credit is not so great
When the world picks your pocket

Live in glass houses
For reality TV to come home

Be yourself in theory
But walk in your parents' shoes

Don't expect inner beauty
To find peace in rawhide skin

Sex is a video game
For you to screw up

Love is myopic
And Cupid needs lasik surgery

Watch out for medics
Who rock aging cradles

Fat happens,
No matter what Atkins says

Your ship sank years ago
And it's time to fly on drugs.

January 2004

48

Queen Bee

The small woman, a mighty conqueror,
Rules from her swivel chair.
She sits tall upon a modern throne,
Holds her telephone receiver like a scepter,
Voices her authority over the loudspeaker
And holds court with peers
Who support her for political gain,
Subordinates for a paycheck.
How she assumed such power
Is not for us to know.
We are not princesses of privilege,
Never attended finishing schools
To learn the secrets of her success.

Never cross her path
For fear that she will turn into a scorpion,
Sting you with lethal poison
Until she annihilates your self-esteem.

Be a follower, not a leader!
Keep your ego bowed when she passes by.
Should you forget,
She will make you pay dearly.

She is our savior and salvation
For our kind to survive in the modern world.
She is responsible for our pittance of honey
Produced from the sweat of our time and brains
As long as we sell our souls to the Devil
Whose bed she keeps warm at night.

Worship in her temple dedicated to herself
Where the high priestess proclaims
Her gospel of greed and selfishness
Throughout the corporate world.

The Queen Bee is too smug
To think that kingdoms come and go.
She will become fresh meat,
An appetizer for someone stronger
Who will smash her idols to smithereens,

Sack her booty of stolen ideas and hard work.
Her once great hive will be no more,
For she will be conquered
Quicker than a corporate microsecond.

August 2000

Truth

Computer screens stare into each other's minds
While pens and pads fall asleep on nostalgic nonsense.
Tensions post desperate messages on cybernetic glass
In a dual of opposites who write in reverse
On keyboards waging an honest battle of the heart.
Rhetoric hastily loses the message upon delivery
Sending time and space into shock therapy,
Trashing truth in the end.

February 2003

The End

In the beginning
There is the alpha,
Sending us out
To conquer the world,
To walk about
Like blindfolded prophets,
Seeking miracles,
Exposing peacock feathers
By predicting oracles,
Pleasing sulfuric dreams
Until we are cured
With visionary disillusionment
When we finish at the omega,
Shunning defeated alpha
In the end.

April 2001

End of an Error

Religion is an addiction
That stirs the masses into losing their minds
To the will of the lord in a paper house
Which collapses around them
In multiple metaphors to stagger
And amuse the imagination.
Where is the logic of life
When struggle demands you to write
In the language of your heart,
Dipped in the ink of your precious blood,
While wearing the yoke of battle
Against the brotherhood of the odds?

You walk slower each day,
Wear meager battlement in a faded blindfold,
Against the edge that confines you
To a boundary allowing no passage
To the promised land of hope
And the vaguer one at the horizon of demise.

Rip the blindfold from your tired eyes
To see the end as your maker.
The firing squad is waiting
For you to escape from an error
Conceived from a persona created by yourself
Outside paper walls of a world
Born out of nothing.

November 2002

Generic Religion

Believe in the unknown,
A triple persona of holiness.
Wash your sins away with extra-strength guilt,
Look immaculate and acceptable for the flock,
But clean up the mess after mass.
Beg forgiveness on Sunday,
Only to be rewarded with regret on Monday.
Your enemies are granted easy pass
After you pay your hard-earned tithe
To God, Uncle Sam, Company,
And to the fifty-two credit card decks
That pump your stomach for their daily bread.

July 2002

God and TV

God sits on a sofa, watching TV,
Eats junk food between commercials.
War bangs on the walls,
The screen shouts back on CNN.
He turns to a sitcom about "Friends"
Asking a "Soprano" to break a leg
By knocking "ER" off the air.
Nearby newspapers kickboxing over candidates,
Turn voters' minds into altered states.
A remote tells God to switch the channel
To watch a single woman have sex - with surgery,
Another commercial offers less carbs for the bucks.
God gets bored, condemns the remote and TV to hell
And finds salvation in a cold can of beer.

June 2004

Chapter 8
Miscellaneous Musings

At the Edge

Indecision thwarts anxious feet
And glues them to the edge.
High above footprints of hesitation
Rests the source of all judgment.

Time's heart beats faster,
Wisdom's blood circulates.
The edge holds its breath
And waits for a decision.

Whatever the outcome,
The feet shall decide.

September 2003

The Empty Hall

Darkness rings my doorbell -
I see only the empty hall
Standing outside,
Whispering to my fear
Of a secret presence here,
Waiting to tilt the equilibrium
Of my tired night.

Yet there is light
Protruding from darkness
According to my flat.
Looking across the empty hall,
There is nothing to fear at all
In the mirror's cool reflection.
Without question or objection,
I must face the fear:
The guilty one is me.

April 2001

Art of Lies

A portrait covers up the blank stare of a canvas
In imaginative shades found in a crayon box.
Layer upon layer, the portrait evolves
While truth remains protected
Under application of paint,
Making it difficult for artificial light
To scrape past the surface.

July 2003

Lost and Found

A blank page has forgotten what was said -
Its inkling of memory has faded from view.
The pen scratches its head,
Cycling on nondescript vellum.
But it too has forgotten what was said.
The writer squirms and wonders why,
Until the moment before comes forward,
Returning what was lost to the rightful owner
When the ink reappears and the message is found.

June 2003

Zero

Sudden emptiness takes you to purgatory
Where the plus and minus divide in debate;
You hide within a circumference of nothingness,
Waiting for time to tip the balance in either direction.

July 2002

54

Special Delivery

Translucent bandages conceal a message
Like ribbons dressed for a surprise,
Waiting for the gifted person to unravel
Anticipation behind paper and promise.
A hostage in the impact of its deliverance
When the unknown emerges from its gut,
Shredding the grin off the ardent face.

September 2003

Egg

Stimulation, an embryonic bird,
Squirms in a karmic nest.
Its fetal mind pierces the dark
And sharpens its beak to peck
At the wall of brittle destiny.
A war is looming outside,
Ready to feast on fresh yolk.
Time grinds into decision -
Hibernation hatches -
The battle must begin.

June 2003

Tears

Innocence reflects my face in the eyes of tears -
Regret falls freely down my cheeks
Imitating the anguish of this passing storm
Which bangs against the windowpane.

I must cry, even as an adult,
As I watch a procession of days carry a casket
Toward the freshly dug soil outside my window.
Minutes clench the hands of hours and seconds,
Listening to months and weeks recite their eulogy
For a year that existed in a comatose question:
"How will it all end?"

But this storm is losing its own battle
And bangs on my windowpane for the last time.
In the distance, I hear human thunder
Emerge, loud and clear, from midnight's womb
And crumble the silence that made me cry.

December 2003

Indigo

Indigo raindrops beat the drum,
Persuade me to take another route
And recapture secrets of a shaman's soul.
I visualize myself in a pool of indigo,
Cleansing evils from my feminine temple.

Music swims in raindrops,
Serenades spirit.
Ancient chakras sing
Without beginning or end.
Different scales rise and fall -
My mood has a lovely voice
And chants about a future
When rainbows will rise from tears.
A warm glow massages silence,
Creation caresses my hands.

My mind resonates energy
And my blood mimics its cycle.
Consecrated thoughts begin to bleed
In words once lost.
The water consumes my passion
As indigo incense burns away the pain
For me to breathe in and swim.

February 2003

The Opening

What is belief when walls seal us in
And windows and doors refuse to budge,
When fear is the other occupant of your time?
This shadow of contradiction trails your mind,
Growing larger by the hour.

Reach out for it, no matter how strong the walls
Or stubborn the framed barriers may seem.
Belief, like the tiniest crack,
Will expand when you least expect it -
The opening will set you free.

March 2002

Random Thoughts

Laughter is the battle cry of humor,
Happiness is the dark side of misery.
Love comes in more calories than ice cream,
Beauty finds her soul mate in the face of ugliness.
Strength comes to no one, and everyone, on Viagra,
Tears wash away the orgasms of Yin and Yang.
Friendship can really sink without the help of ice,
Truth walks incognito, wearing a shadow of lies.
Progress discriminates against healthy turds,
Sanity is the natural-born mother of craziness.
Numbers lose count calculating the logic of idiots,
Myths come to life when drugs blow them to the wind.
Musings promise and do nothing to protect the innocent,
Random thoughts amuse questions without answers.

June 2003

Final Words

Sun departs and horizon disappears from sight

A door closes and the last petal falls to the floor

A song sings its final note and music goes deaf

Rooms lie still and time speaks to their silence

Sleep takes up residence and words are no more.

October 2002

Alphabetical
Appendix

Alphabetical Appendix

Art of Lies	- July 2003	Page 54
The Asylum	- March 2001	Page 47
At the Edge	- September 2003	Page 53
Baby Dolls	- May 2003	Page 27
Blessed Stranger	- December 2002	Page 19
Blue Fire	- October 2003	Page 2
The Bride Wore Black	- February 2004	Page 7
Crucifixion	- August 2002	Page 41
The Dance	- January 2003	Page 20
Daydreams	- July 2002	Page 41
Dead Flower	- February 2002	Page 25
Dirty Secret	- March 2003	Page 9
Dirty Trick	- September 2003	Page 11
The Door	- April 2003	Page 40
Dreamscape	- October 2002	Page 43
Egg	- June 2003	Page 55
The Elastic Canvas	- November 2000	Page 35
Emptiness	- January 2004	Page 3
The Empty Hall	- April 2001	Page 53
The End	- April 2001	Page 50
End of an Error	- November 2002	Page 51
Erased By Myself	- January 2003	Page 23
Eternal Sleep	- September 2000	Page 37
The Eyes of Love	- January 2004	Page 15
Final Words	- October 2002	Page 59
Fire	- June 2004	Page 34
Fit for a Child	- September 2003	Page 26
Flying	- March 2003	Page 12
Forgotten Child	- November 2002	Page 25
Generic Religion	- July 2002	Page 52
God and TV	- June 2004	Page 52
The Goddess	- June 2000	Page 45
The Golden Door	- December 2004	Page 30
Hello	- February 2002	Page 6
The Hole	- September 2002	Page 39
Honesty	- May 2002	Page 9
Humoresque	- March 2003	Page 42
In Death's Bed	- December 2001	Page 29
Indigo	- February 2003	Page 57
Instant Coffee	- September 2003	Page 47
The Ivory Tower	- May 2003	Page 2
The Lioness	- January 2002	Page 33

Alphabetical Appendix continued

Little Girls	- May 2005	Page 45
Lost and Found	- June 2003	Page 54
Metamorphosis	- March 2003	Page 13
Normal People	- July 2002	Page 12
Observation Deck	- February 2003	Page 24
The Opening	- March 2002	Page 58
Phoenix of Light	- November 2003	Page 38
The Pixie	- October 2002	Page 18
PMS Pizza	- October 2004	Page 14
The Puppeteer	- October 2000	Page 1
Put Your Head Inside Your Heart	- April 2002	Page 19
Queen Bee	- August 2000	Page 49
Rage	- June 2004	Page 10
Random Thoughts	- June 2003	Page 58
Revenge	- August 2002	Page 11
Revolution	- July 2000	Page 31
Scars	- October 2003	Page 23
Secrets	- August 2002	Page 5
Sensuality	- May 2005	Page 4
Simplicity	- July 2002	Page 46
Special Delivery	- September 2003	Page 55
The Spiral	- November 2002	Page 47
Stain	- March 2003	Page 6
Teardrops on My Pillow	- October 2002	Page 24
Tears	- December 2003	Page 56
Tell Me a Story	- November 2003	Page 46
Tenderness in Reverse	- September 2003	Page 12
Tension	- January 2004	Page 48
Touched By a Guide	- January 2003	Page 10
Truth	- February 2003	Page 50
Twilight	- September 2001	Page 40
Twins	- January 2003	Page 31
Universe In Motion	- August 2002	Page 16
Unknown Minutes	- December 2001	Page 36
The Valley of Sorrows	- June 2000	Page 28
Vixen in the Rough	- January 2002	Page 21
Vocal Minds	- June 2002	Page 34
X	- January 2002	Page 32
Yo Soy Una Persona Aislada	- June 2002	Page 17
Zero	- July 2002	Page 54